T0149144

# Heaven's Gate

Also by **Tony Curtis**

Poems:
Album
Preparations
Letting Go
Selected Poems
Taken for Pearls
War Voices
The Last Candles
The Arches (with collages by John Digby)
Dal Confine (Selected Poems in Italian)

Criticism:
How to Study Modern Poetry
How Poets Work (ed)
Welsh Painters Talking
Welsh Artists Talking
The Art of Seamus Heaney (ed)
Assemblea di Poeti (Anglo-Welsh poems in Italian) (ed)
Wading Through Deep Water (Parkinson's Disease Society)

Anthologies:
The Poetry of Snowdonia
The Poetry of Pembrokeshire
Love from Wales
Coal

# Heaven's Gate
# Tony Curtis

seren

seren

is the book imprint of
Poetry Wales Press Ltd
Nolton Street, Bridgend, Wales
www.seren-books.com

ISBN 1-85411-2945

A CIP record for this title is available from the British Library.

The publisher acknowledges the financial assistance
of the Arts Council of Wales.

Printed by Bell and Bain, Glasgow.

Cover: Ernest Zobole: Painting about Penrhys & Ystrad, April, 1997.

Back cover author portrait by James Donovan.

# Contents

# Heaven's Gate

*for Dannie and Joan Abse*

Outside the Mughal Emperor in the sharp air
under a sky precise as a map
we point at Hale Bopp and its final, slow
splash out of our world into the depthless dark.
Full up with lamb pasanda, chicken jalfrezi
and puffed, sweet nan, we couldn't be
more earth-bound, more remote from flight.

There they go,
the thirty-three California crazies
who gave up on our century.
They're dead as dodos sailing through heaven's gate
in the gas stream of the comet
with their personal guides, the aliens.

While we, full of wind and spice, look
up from the jammed tight car park,
without envy or scorn,
but warm in friendship and food
and the pleasure of living this night
six million by six million miles below
the chaos of the gas and rock that now,
just now, completes this perfect sky
with a painter's smear of titanium white.

# Icarus

Out of an English summer morning's sky
drops an Indian who failed in flight
miles short of heaven. This frozen Icarus
thrown from the wheel-bay of a 747
splashes into a Surrey reservoir,
cracking the water like a whip.

This poor man stowed away
in the Delhi heat, curled
himself into an oven of rubber and oil,
and dreamed as he rose in the deafening take-off
of food and rain and *Coca Cola*
and television where the colour never ends.

The waitress at the Granada stop
tapping in two coffees and a Danish
at the till, for no reason at all,
looked up, saw a bird, or an engine,
or a man, and then nothing
but blue sky again.

# Letters to Gareth in Amherst

## I

One of those grey weeks with nothing much to say.
Late September — the beginnings of serious rain.
Fitful days. Longer nights of tv. (City lost again)
and new runs of sitcoms; the odd play
that sparks, but Potter's dead and the sharp
wit of the golden age has paled. Before your time.
The last thing you want to hear is us carp
about Welsh weather. The autumn I'm
seeing in the Vale is hardly the Fall of New England,
but there's two beeches by the thirteenth green
that are flickering into flame — yellow and red. And
yesterday on our grass near the cherry stumps we've seen
a plump, young woodpecker straight off the cider flagon
feeding, courtesy of my final cut of the lawn.

## II

I've felled the cherry in the back yard
we thought we'd have both set to earlier, back
in the summer. Its leafless, dead wood that marred
our view across to England was brittle and cracked.
I worked to angle it away from shrubs and the ivied wall,
the purple hydrangea, that root of holly your mother's
planted. The outer branches would easily fall,
but at the trunk I could have used another's
hands and weight. The chainsaw's angle left
my writing hand's index finger raw.
A crucifixion of cherry remained. I worked and cleft
it down to three short trunks. Then, Henry Moore,
I saw that sea-curved Pembrokeshire rock we'd kept when
you were ten, would balance there, and polish in the rain.

## III

I thought I'd keep you in touch with the sport
this year away in New England — with your Red Sox,
Patriots, that grid-iron football: the American sort
of self-referential crap — faded-star commentators on the box
for their Super Bowl, their O.J., their Opens closed,
their experts who call up bewildering stats
to constantly punctuate the practised, posed
camera-conscious "Hi, Mom!" bits. But I see that's
too distant now for you to care, too Welsh, too petty.
Still, in Cardiff Saturday-night, drunks rolled past us
                                       in celebration
of another Steve Robinson knock-out victory.
At the Arms Park, Ieuan's broken ankle felled a nation.
And the newspaper placards still proclaim our certain crash —
*Wales Star Goes North*. They sell our dreams for cash.

# IV

While Bron was being interviewed at Clare,
I walked the Backs and paid to sit
In King's College Chapel. If man's celestial need encloses air
And shapes a special place from stone and glass and wit,
Then none excels Wastell's soaring fan vault,
The whole arched magnificence finished by a screen of oak
That bloated, eighth Henry gave, and Anne Boleyn whose fault
Was to displeasure him. Her white neck stained the block.
There's blood, no doubt, on art that celebrates and saves —
Ruben's solid, fleshy, stagy Adoration,
The organ's apocalyptic bellow crashing in waves
Of need and praise over choir and congregation.
Fellows in Clare with frayed pullovers, decide your sister's fate:
The privileged faith of another age, uplifts, distracts me while
                                                                    I wait.

# V

Thought I'd better write a letter — *So What* —
Tell you all about the weather — *So What* —
I'm listening to Miles Davis, that magic
Jazz-horn Mozart of our too slick, synthesised age —
*So What* — its insistent, two-note tick
That sticks in the brain. You say you've seen Dylan on stage —
He was acoustic, The Man, a 60s has-been you used to hate.
Then, in Amherst, James Taylor live, mellow and so what
If he's my age and Mum's. Your view from the Empire State
Was clear for 25 Manhattan miles? Soon you'll be locked in tight
By snow in your cabin-fevered dorm. Winter's closing in,
Your Christmas will be white, and some. So what can you do
But play American tunes, the anthems for where we've all been.
Wrap warm and stay cool, son. Book that flight — we miss you.

## VI

This is just to say our visit was fine
— Thank everyone for the typical American hospitality —
And that we're safely home and back in the old routine.
Though we were delayed at JFK, and I wobbled a bit. Three
Gins saw me through the turbulence and darkness.
At Heathrow, behind us there was a flurry and a lot
Of fuss and Paul & Linda and the kids came through.
                                        Who'd guess
The Dakota had ever happened? The films I shot
Came out fine and that one from the yellow cab
Of the sidewalk where Lennon was killed
Is sharp and sunny. You and I perched on that slab
Of John's rusting Chevy Malibu hood on Long Island
Is a posey classic. And the green, smooth, whale's-tooth stone
You picked from Jones Beach is on your bedroom sill, at home.

## VII

When you're back home you'll see the Irishmen
Have caught me with their black-stuff patter, "Do you
A fine job, Sor, we will. Best stuff only, then."
The sons of the sons of the sons of the crew
That built Victorian England's roads, burrowed under London.
This new-laid drive would never set in your Deep South —
Alabama, Mississippi, under their torturing sun.
You say there's a red-neck culture still. So mind your mouth,
Eyes open and take it all in. We're glad you've cut your hair
For the land of *Easy Rider*, tar-baby, Graceland and lynchings.
Nothing's black and white simple, as you're learning there.
Difference is what makes us what we are. My new kerbing's
Loose but we'll not see the Galway boys back. Cash in hand. Gone.
This hot June, on both continents we need a settling rain.

# The Doctors Weiss on First Avenue

From the nineteenth floor
this life almost lived through seems good
in the late afternoon
with the sun's aureole a warm muffler
around the streets below 23rd
and the twin slabs of the World Trade Center.

"From here," he says, "I can still see
the lower East Side where I was born
and grew, the high school and the NYU;
the Dental School where Irma scared ten
sorts of commotion into forty years' Chemistry
classes, scattered now across the world
and all of them rich, and some of them
dead."

       Irma's in her chair and moves
little without the hired nurse
who's left early today for her sick mother
in Brooklyn across the river.
From the three sides of this apartment
the city rushes with purpose into the night,
the blare of horns and brakes in the canyons
below the secret lives of flat roofs
with their water tanks and elevator gear.

"I remember the excitement when the Flatiron
rose up twenty or so storeys," she says,
"between the Doughboys parade and the '29 Crash.
That's all lost down there
in the high-rise of 23rd and the avenues."

The collections of two lives —
the inscribed club-head for his hole-in-one
twenty years ago out at Massapequa;
the open Torah on its stand.
The certificates and plaques in the American way
of commemoration — President of the Temple,
the citations of their students.
The etching of a mother and child
by Mary Cassatt, light and tender and firm.

These two lives, rooted in the pogroms
of Hungary and the Ukraine,
have grown to purpose and respect
at the end of this botched century
with its marvels and crimes.
And from the nineteenth floor today
the view is fine.

He leads us around the house plants,
"Step this way through the jungle,"
to view the rival towers —
the Chrysler and the Empire State raised platforms
and aerials until they both got tired and were dwarfed
by dozens of cloud scrapers in the post-war booms.
The late orange rinds of the Chrysler's deco swirls
become its night lights.

                And as the Empire State
tonight chooses blue and white at its pinnacle,
we are not sure whether it's for another
promise of peace in Palestine and Israel,
or the Yankees' whitewash of the Padres,
their twenty-fourth World Series.

For this is the world if you want to believe it
and the canyon of heroes snowed tickertape
this morning on the victory parade,
Wall Street did a little trade,
and for another day this city
seemed like the whole world:
from the skaters in the Park
to the Senegalese street sellers
of fake and hot Gucci and Chanel;
from the steamed duck of the Tang Pavilion
to the snatched subway bagels with a schmear.

# California Burning

The pool ripples red
under a black and grey sky.

This is a nightmare at mid-day,
one long exhalation as the country burns.

White walls are graffitied with smoke;
The End announced by each burning bush.

The pool furniture re-arranges itself
into a group of reclining figures.

The windows are stained glass,
then crack. The tapestried drapes

unravel, their patterns unpicked into gold threads.
The suite smells of burned animals.

Les Beigneurs enter the river.
Portraits weep, then picasso themselves.

The one abandoned car cooks
then demolishes the garage.

The roof shuffles its pack
and slaps its hand down noisily on the table.

Some say a careless camper;
some say a freak

with the sort of eyes that flame
behind dark glasses.

Along the block, one white house
stands untouched behind its bank of ice-plants:

the heat squeezes their water
and quenches itself elsewhere.

This is how the dreams burn,
the lies we compose play themselves out.

All the ease that money can buy
crinkles like old bank-notes in a furnace.

# In Cambridge, Mass.

From our rented basement on Ellery
we tour Harvard Square for records and books.
In the Fogg, Monets shine with a wet, light nowness.

We ride the T inbound — to Boston Common
where Colonel Shaw and his Negroes still
fix their faces on freedom,
and then the train runs on to the MFA.
In Delvaux's *The Salute* the clerk raises
his bowler hat to a classical beauty
revealed as her garments fall.
The street sideways watches it all.

Back on relaxed Ellery Street
little moves and no-one watches.

Guy and Philip, the gays I had imagined
from our phone booking,
are a married couple in their sixties —
he is a retired law teacher, she
a Ph.D from the Sorbonne who's found art
and then philosophy, part-time,
across three decades.

Her space-to-let is a gallery
because here everyone does something else
as well as what they do.

Our basement flat shows her collages
and wall hangings —
thick falls of wool and hemp
bursting like guts out of the walls.

In a skylight at the grass level
— a space you can't access —
she has arranged a cable-wire spool table
with two carved decoy ducks,
six conches in a line, old white sponges,
a twist of huge, orange sea rope,
a marker buoy circled by bleached and aged coconuts.

From Mexico to Cape Cod to Maine
bits of the world she's brought home.
Which is what we all do,
assembling the pieces which give us weight
and validate the times we've seen,
the memories of where we've been
that might make us shine.

# The Eighth Dream

First he fingers wet sand into the names —
his hand traces the letters, then the numbers
of the squadron, then the boy's home state.
Sand spills into other names and numbers
above and below. He wipes the line
smooth with a sponge; then with an artist's brush
flicks away the final lodged grains.

This is the way to raise the dead
for the photograph the relatives receive.
It is fifty years and those who remembered
have phoned or faxed for flowers to be laid:
a wreath under one of the columns of the dead
where the long-lost brother holds his place
in the alphabet of the missing.

It is the end of the first week of December —
a brushing of snow highlights the grass
and softens the Portland stone walls of remembrance.
The rectangular ponds have coffin-lids of ice.
The stars and stripes is moulded to its towering pole,
the point from which the headstones radiate
their Roman Crosses and Stars of David.

These are the boys whose masks were torn apart,
whose blood froze in the high air over Berlin,
Dresden and Cologne, whose minced bodies were
                                    hosed out
over the warm fuselage in a Cambridgeshire field.
The ones who died slowly by an open window, listening
to strange birdsong. Those who ploughed into the
                                    runway fog.
Sailors who gagged on diesel and salt in the dark
Atlantic, and were numbed out of life.
They were the numbers on the walls
behind the Enigma boffins, Christ's and King's men
unscrambling the alphabet in Bletchley's Nissen huts.

Eighth Air Force fliers had a target of missions
that shifted — twenty, thirty, thirty-five —
always away from them as targets and statistics
were chalked across the wall of the hut.
Write it down, write it down.
They used their *Zippos* to burn the pub's ceiling,
memorials of crashed numbers of friends.

# The Wheelbarrow

*for Kevin Sinnott*

After a soaking day the new lambs
come out of their huddle
and are tugging milk from their mother
faster than they can graze.
It is surely the cusp of spring,
the last wet burden winter makes us bear.

*This winter, just after we'd moved in,*
*we had a mishap with the dog*
*they'd left us with this place.*
*A fine guard dog —*
*named after a German city.*
*But it got out and mauled some sheep.*

In the still-wet painting he is pushing the dead
weight of it up the slope deeper into the trees.
His father-in-law has attached a rope to the barrow
and puts his weight into the pull.

It is all dark browns and greens
in the blackness of the woods
where they will dig a grave.
He does not tell me if words were said,
and I will not give them voices.

Now with the lambs in the valley
milky and spring-frisky
the big painting seems a memorial
of some distant, forgotten war.
This work he will not sell, but hang here
in their church-in-a-house
with its arched windows and great curved beams.

That rainy, winter night
I see them spading down the covering
of earth, needles and leaf-mulch.
Then one of them, or both of them, sings,
or cries. Or it might be the rain
in the trees and in their eyes.

## Survivors

It is countless suns and moons
since everything changed.

Now there are small groups
of brittle survivors

with the blue and ochre skin,
their gas-masks, rags of clothes.

They have mastered the science of thongs —
any skin, stripped, twisted and dried.

These strap their quivers,
but there are so few arrows,

and much of the day is spent
searching for wood, uncharred,

long enough to shape a bow.
Tins are growing scarce, and soon

they will vote again to risk the masks.
The days are going, and at least

if it is the end, faces, red and marked,
will loosen back into whoever they were.

# Faces

This is the last
the very last,
the fifteenth, sixteenth.
I don't choose to count:
each face different and the same.

The still-born, the late miscarriage,
the tiny death in the incubator,
tubes removed, the support switched off.

Each imagined face I re-imagine
for the almost parents —
the Obstets people and the counsellors
are sure it helps, fixes the grief,
focuses the love.

Each failed foetus, each shrivelled life
I father-forth with paints.

Are these portraits kept private in drawers
for the special times, anniversaries,
when the pain becomes unbearable,
or are they mantelpiece, front-room wall
displayed — a sort of shared conversation of pain?

I have to stop
to move back to my own life and vision,
for the ghosts I have conjured,
float in my dreams,
ripped untimely from me.

These I never show my wife, my children.
I feel some sort of betrayal is close.
I don't want complexion, nose,
hair to take anything from my own,
these poor dead things.

# Visitors

To the bestiary of our garden
we add this.

To the flitting of sparrows and thrushes,
the raucous strutting of the magpie
we add this,

to chaffinches and robin,
to the curled hedgehog in the sodden
chaotic bonfire of cherry branches.

Add this to the evening-golden fox,
street-wise, brushing past
the clean shirts and sheets.

To the dark cloud of starlings, Hitchcock extras,
gorging from the plump, bleeding elderberry,
before wintering south.

Our new season's pair of collared doves,
plumped and pert, chalk-soft, landing
like finest lace handkerchiefs on the lawn.

We add this to the bestiary
of moths, our neighbours' damson-drunk bees.
The green woodpecker that stabbed
at the darkness under our Norway spruce.

Include the bizarre blue and yellow
splash of an escaped parrot, absurd,
forlorn, bedraggled in the stark pear tree
on a drenched day it would not survive.

And from a back window,
looking up from the washing machine,
today we add,

regal on the curved Pembrokeshire beach boulder
I balanced on the lopped cherry stumps,
this peregrine, motionless, staring out
at the stilled and suddenly vacant garden,

dappled flight turned to stone,
holding its breath for a long minute
in which all that moves
is one bright, steel eye
for each half of the universe.

Until the falcon launches itself up
and over our high roof, away
into the rest of the world.

# Down the Road

After the months of standing empty
next door's been bought —
builders' vans parked outside for weeks,
white plastic windows are going up;
the metal frames they've taken out
are stacked inside the stone wall like broken spectacles.
The stucco's painted white.

Miss John left last year after a second break-in —
kids probably, drugs probably — the young copper said.
Right through her house and into her bedroom
for thirty quid.

We've visited her twice in Orchard House
where, "It's nice enough,
not like a hospital."

In the early hours, in the afternoons,
false alarms trigger from houses
up and down the road.
Electric faults, too much rain,
too much sun, cowboy fitters.

Approaching a restless fifty,
for the first time in years
we talk of moving.

The traffic's become a flood.
Crisp bags, drinks cans, cigarette packs
litter the hedge and lawn from schoolboys
and college apprentices training to be cowboys.
Signs and niggles.

As I towel myself in the bathroom
a Tesco bag caught high
in what was Miss John's sycamore
flickers and waves in the sky.
Through the frosted glass it could be the moon
or a white flag.

## Last Things

There will be last things
and some that we know to be the last things.
The photograph at the Falls, once only
the stony faces of the Presidents, the whale's fin
that knifes the green sea and then is gone.

The putt that never dropped
is always followed by the one that does.
Round and around until the heart winds down or bursts.
The last hole, the last card you'll mark.
Your hard-won ticket to the big match that seems now
too far, too noisy, too much trouble.
The ace that scuffed the chalk on, or was
it near, the line in a distant semi-final.

And what of the people?
The four-poster and the acolytes,
the family bedside goodbyes,
the tears of departure, the long, last gaze,
the hands on the cooling hand.
Staged finales that complete the play.
The need to remember that last phone call,
when the weather was shared and another week
passed without distinction.

The paint within the frame holds for us
that face, the valley's season,
the mountains in rain last winter,
and is the marvellous trick of suspension.
The smile, the light alive on water,
the impossible, essential moment around which all this,
a life, might be seen to turn.

Ah, the impatient ones
who choose their time and place —
the locked garage, a journey into bitter blue clouds,
or the passing into the eye of a needle.
And this man, his wife and daughter
sprawled in the kitchen, stands on the cliff-top
looking at the last grey ocean, and at dawn
as the waves draw their first white lines,
walks into them through a hundred feet of air.

## The Last Night at Lydstep

And this one
like an animal
wanted to be alone.

As if his final breaths might
shake another's world,
as if all that a life composed
would collapse before others.

On into the night he worked at his bench.
Was there a caravan step to fix?
Some cupboard lock that would not close?
A faulty bracket he filed in the vice?

Whatever. Through the open
window of the repair shed
the sea breathed for him,
the ocean's exhalation and suck
after its Atlantic marathon.
While his one good lung wheezed
its torn bellows under the glare of a bare bulb.

Useless the hands' work
as the night slid towards him,
and he measured his years
in the guts of cars, the rusty undersides
of chassis and wing —
all dumped in the memory
with the acid tubs in their straw baskets,
the coils of wire, the oily crypts
he descended to raise a claw of light
beneath the road-shitten patina of miles.

All that fixing of things —
coil and dynamo, battery, alternator,
his apprenticeship, the war, a wife, a son,
then debt and disappointments,
a dulling of the spirit despite
the constant green shimmer of shaping fields,
Carmarthenshire, Pembrokeshire,
and the great blue slabs of beyond —
all held in the shortened journey
of his smoked and cracked body.

Tonight clouds close over from the west
and the stars disappear.
Again the sea — always and forever the sea
with its careless knocking
at the fretted caverns
that smoothes the pebbles
each one against the others.

# Wearing the Trousers

A heavy green check
too long in the leg,
too loose at the waist,
flared and dated.
I could wear them for golf
or gardening, I'd said,
saving them from the bundle
my mother had parted with.

Fifteen years hanging from a hook
on the back wall of my wardrobe
behind the clothes I wear:
it's little enough, but keeps me
in touch with him.
I try them on in the mirror —
the legs too long, but now
the waist's quite snug.

Thirteen years short of the mark
he made, I'm going on —
steady, pacing myself to the line.
Taking drink in moderation, I've never smoked,
avoiding the same mistakes.
By such prudence, and luck, we etch the final date.
It still comes to knife, bed, pain,
hitting the floor, pyjamas soiled. Wait.

# At the Water's Edge

After the swordplay with his walking stick,
after the calendar collapsed,
after the garage was locked and the car
driven away by his son,
long after the smutty asides, the accusations
that his wife of sixty years was seeing
the head of Physics long dead,
shortly after the raged throwing of the tea set,
the two-year long sleepy day ending.
Interference. The pictures fuzzy and fading.

He remembers rising from the settee
to stand for the Queen;
one of the school field smokers he caned,
who became a Professor of Law;
and a pretty, young teacher of cookery.
From his armchair in the Water's Edge
he can see the Channel and the Somerset hills.
The tanker like a painted ship
waiting for the tide, or the fall of night
when its waste can be leaked into the sea.

# Blackberries at Pwllcrochan

I drive through Rhoscrowther, through rain.
The refinery has dwarfed the village —
two dozen houses, the church and its graves
under the lea of the hill.
Oil buys out the houses, one by one,
boarded up and numbered for demolition,
as death, job, despair or the money pushes people out.

Those miles of Texaco pipes, barbed fence,
it all goes out of sight as I turn back
down the tunnelled lane to Pwllcrochan —
the church deconsecrated,
boarded-up school and bricked-blind house.
I pull in beside the flattened Rectory's ground
as the security jeep passes by on its round.

The stone barn seems smaller now, and where
that tangled bank of blackberries thicken,
there was the old Rectory, my uncle's. I remember it
huge, too big to fit this space. Here
the kitchen, with its cosy, constant Aga,
potatoes fresh from their fields rattling in the pan,
warm milk and roasted, earthy chickens.
My auntie gave suck at that table,
her great breast singled like a moon.

This is one of the places it begins,
the diaspora of feelings.

Under this pressed earth, was the cellar —
stacked seed potatoes, wrinkled, their eyes on stalks,
and the oily generator my father drove us down for,
weekends of tinkering, conjuring the pulsing light.
And there, higher than that sycamore,

the bedrooms where my cousins and I were tucked
in for the long, name-calling, tumbling nights.
In the disappeared orchard
we climbed and swung for apples;
we forked at rats in the barn's back stores.

Now and here it starts,
the weighing of the heart.

The rain chills my face and neck.
It sweeps from the west, blearing the hard
gleam of the massive pipes and tanks
where Bummer George's wood has been sliced
out of the land. The wet gusts carry
the dull, metalled workings of the refinery.

I start to pick the plump, washed, blackberries.
In my cupped hands they have the weight
of blown birds' eggs, and their seedy,
sweet music plays in the mouth.

# Ernie's House

*Ernest Zobole: "The later perspective is a tyranny."*

There is always the man
in the house
with his easel.

His wife and dog are also in the house
but may not always be seen.

The house looks over a valley
down which the river slides
to the sea.

It has been coal-black and bitter,
but now salmon muscle against its blue-black flow.

The valley is terraced with houses
that are growing empty.

The hills hunch their shoulders
and wait to be counted.

More often than not it is
night. Stars. More stars.

The lights of cars explode,
the street-lamps come into bloom.
The graveyard's crosses glint.

Far off, at sea, ships
on their way to everywhere else.

# Looking into the Field

From the five corners of the field
they lift their heads and move towards him.
This is the man who brings food.
His collie presses against the window
of the Land Rover and leaves a nose-round watermark.
He walks to the four stiff legs of a dead sheep
and bends to grasp fistfuls of tight wool.
Lifting from his knees he pulls and rolls
the ewe upright, setting the legs kicking again.
Tubful of life, she bleats and waddles to new grass.
The field has been put to rights and as he walks back
his flock return to their grass and the first autumn leaves.
Four disappointed crows flap into the sky she'd
stared up through like a cloudy blue tunnel.

# Autumn in the Kitchen

Autumn's in the kitchen
chopping garlic and peppers,
soaking chickpeas in the large pan.
She says she's not rigid —
her plants and cures are complementary,
a rotting appendix still needs the knife.
We are, of course, what we eat;
tonight we are having bake with couscous.

As she takes up another garlic
and splits the crown with her fingers,
she begins to share her litanies of healing:
pulsatilla — wind flower for childbirth,
when a woman's funny, angry, mystical,
or belladona when you're red in the face, pained,
and camomilla for teething and labour.
The flue is blocked with old nests —
your marriage is not flowing.
The cistern floods when your lover
boils over? Well, water is the element
associated with feelings. Fire —
the passions themselves.

                    And for burns?
Honey.
Two fingers in the jar, then spread
it smoothly over the wound.
She must move in a world of such potency,
weeds grow for us, bees fly
their armies of sweet assault
to feed and soothe all of us.
And the whole garden of the world
tends not to itself, but to us
and moves with us as we move.

# The Yoke

*i.m. Gertrude Hermes*

See the world as an egg
moving out of darkness
into what might be the light.

The harlequin bird is all lines
and angles, sharp jointed
and hard ribbed in a closed
sea of cells and ribbons of life
pulsing against the edges
of what may live.

This matter yoked to the cross
of back and wings is crucified
and longs to fly.

Here it all begins
at the centre of possibility
seeded and locked, the law, the joke,
the one that could soar
out into the spoiled universe.
The one we wait for.

# House of Cards

*for Sally Moore*

The afternoon stretches like a cat.
They wait.
One looks out to sea
beyond the lighthouse and the cliffs
to the world of ships.

The black king is trapped
in a corner of the dead board.
Ten to two.
The floor tiles gleam,
the plants have been watered,
the memory of coffee in the mouth
furs against the tongue.

Once again she builds the house
of cards, triangles on triangles.
She makes three levels
using only the numbers.
There are no Kings, Queens or Jacks.

*What do you see?*
    *Nothing. The sea. Clouds.*
*Look. Look, turn around*
*before they topple.*
The afternoon stretches.
There is nothing to do
but wait and shuffle the cards.

# Lottie Stafford's neck

Morning sunlight catching
the heat of her like sex.
The way the light glazes her neck
at that moment she turns,
her hands gripping the washing tub,
as Jenny comes down the stairs with
the bedding across her shoulders
in a fluster of gossip.

That shining, taut slope of skin
Sir William caught with his brushes,
a scene from the mind,
the life of service he imagined.
Hours in his studio after work
her neck craned and stiffening
while the gas-light came and went
with the breeze of evening.

To be finished on her Sunday off
when she straightened from the pose
and walked around to his side.
And afterwards she drank his tea,
put on her coat and went back to the big house,
her room in the attic.
Or sipped tea
and did not put on her coat.

# English Oaks

While the remarkable child plays the latest sonata
Admiral Collingwood excuses himself
and takes the air, out over the lawn,
beyond the Duke's Italian gardens
to the English woods.
It is his custom to stop at intervals,
as if listening to birdsong,
but from the pockets of his breeches
he drops, one by one, the acorns he's brought.

The music now is fitful and barely heard
on the sou' sou' easterly as it rises
to set the trees groaning and panting.
He sees masts of single pine,
the wooden walls of England,
decks of elm, and from each acorn
he presses into grass between the ferns
the keels of the fleet will grow.
There among the buttercups, cowslips,
and the white stars of wild garlic,
England's men'o war will be seeded
for the sons of his sons.

He treads into rain-softened earth the last one
and slaps his gloves on his leg.
It is a beginning.
The rookery, startled into life, rises
and blackens the sky like a broadside
of shot taken high in the rigging.

# The Digger

It were at Naseby Fight we turned the King's tide
and laid out square the side of Parliament.
Taking up our lines
tight along the Sulby hedge,
we thought to be secure.
But Rupert's horse pushed back our left
and nearly turned us inside out.
Then Oliver's horse did the self same thing
to their left and snapped shut
the flank like a mouse-trap —
Fairfax and Cromwell and us dragoons
over Rupert, Digby and the King.

But in the praise of the Lord
and good Cromwell's Model Army
what dreams of a new order I hold
are soured by presences
that sweat me night on night.

For their baggage, scattered after the disarray,
we caught in the open on the Leicester road
with its gabbling sluts, as we saw.
Those of no rank we held
and put to the blade,
giving them the nose and cheeks of whores.
The King's letters had discovered
his call for foreign papists to strengthen his cause —
and we took them for the Irish followers of camp.
When now I know that they were poor Welsh
and in their tongue called for mercy
that was strange to our ears.
We split the nose and sliced the cheeks
and thought to show them the Lord's right judgement.
Their skirts were shitten with fear.

Now I dig for the new order of things
and slice the earth for the fruit of labour.
When I do stretch up from the spade
I love the clean wind that clears the runnels
of sweat from my face. War
I put behind me.
Through the trees I sometimes hear
the wind give witness to the Lord
in tongues.

# Mametz

As the schoolchildren move in knots and lines
from Petersen's brash memorial dragon
to the curved promontory of Mametz Wood
they stumble and slow to a hushed walk
over the ploughed earth,
with the memory of machine guns
hammering in their ears.

I pick up a gnarled knuckle-bone of flint —
grey-white, it shows a dark, hard blue when split.
Imagine the earth showering this stuff as each shell
blew the Royal Welch's ranks apart.
Of such stuff are honourable side-shows made.

The Queen of the Wood's craters have grown lush
as lovers' bowers, softened by ferns and grasses.
Two rusted, stubbed shells that died in flight
now lie like logs. And the trees
in their last leaves of this eightieth year
flaunt silver, brown and green from the rich earth:
Sion and Billy Crower and Emil
and Aneirin and Dai Great-coat.

At every crossroad on the Somme
the December harvest piles a Golgotha of sugar beet.
In the corner bar in Bapaume
the croissants turn to butter on the tongue
and the coffee is strong and sweet.

# From the New House

We have cleared his last bedroom.
Through the curved sweep of the bay windows
the sun is dropping over the edge of the Llŷn,
its final minutes illuminating
the darkening sea, the mountains of Snowdonia.

At Berchesgarden Herr Hitler showed us
the view from a window so vast it was as if the Alps
had been brought to the largest cinema screen,
whiter than any other white, the peaks
catching at clouds. Between the two main slopes,
fixed as in the sights of a rifle, his Austria.

We were wined and dined and talked
of the Great War and of the new world to be built,
the corporal and the Prime Minister,
both statesmen now, you might say.

They drove us down their wide, white concrete roads
to Munich where LL.G. laid a wreath at the Soldier's Tomb
and the Martyrs' monument for his revolution, 1923.
In fifteen years these roads unrolled
like cloth across their country,
and overhead other roads on bridges
like so many arches of triumph. Autobahn
highroads pushing through reclaimed land
into a future my cine camera caught
over the gleaming bonnet of our Mercedes car.

Formal, upright as their constant raised-arm salutes,
these people, LL.G. remarked to me, were undefeated
in their spirit. The Fuehrer, though, fidgeted much
and at dinner was somewhat ill-at-ease. Still,
the man was surely leading a nation into the light.
When LL.G. passed on we drew this curtain
on a world he could see was coming out of that darkness,
peace no more than six months away.

He travelled down Tŷ Newydd drive to the Dwyfor's
banks on a flat farm cart strewn with flowers
pulled by working horses.
And the people filled the hedges and ditches
crying as he passed. And as he passed
his people, the men's arms raised to lift slow hats
off their bare, bowed heads.

## Marini's Riders

They hold to their stone horses
like life-rafts
these riders.

Perched on a plinth,
astride a wave,
balanced on a ledge

they are arrested in the panting,
rearing or wresting of a ride
in the world. Oh, Riders

fool themselves
when their knees and hands
hold these horses to some

journey they think they know.
Riders are carried high and mighty
away with their precarious power,

which is why Peggy
in her Venice mansion
used her Marini Rider

customised by the sculptor
to take any one
of a set of pricks.

She would choose the size
according to her guests' sensibilities
and fit the horse to effect.

See, as the servants prepare
for the meal, her finger runs
over the case of horse tools.

The Rider keeps to his
course. There is nothing
he can do.

# Sunday Morning in Alba

In the baroque, overbearing darkness
of the brick church, what first strikes one
are the fourteen heads of Christ,
each angled in a different station of pain,
life-size, but body-less on its small cross.
The whole crucifixion quoted in parts.

This is the church of Margherita di Savoia
who, seven centuries ago,
gave her life to save unfortunates
from cold, hunger and eternal darkness.
Now we see —
she lies in a glass-sided coffin
they have raised to the height of an altar.
No effigy this, in renewed habits
she is actual flesh, time-shrivelled,
her tiny bones held in tautened, dark skin.

Each time lira are dropped into the slot
an electric candle comes on.
There are eight this evening,
randomly lit.
There is no flame or smell,
no down-folding of wax.
As night draws down,
silently, in turn,
they go out.

# The Break

After the rumour about taxi drivers,
each time they leave for the station
or the airport, they perform
the same ritual — turning round from the car
and waving at the net curtains.

Then the conversation:
"I still feel strange letting someone use our place."
Or, "Jane will feed and let out the cat, won't she?"

In the emptiness of their house only
the dust moves in its draughty waltz through the air.
The photographs of their grown-up children
at graduation, the grandchild's first walk.
A pair of watercolours, 1886, of mountains in Wales.
That lustre jug from her grandmother's farm.
The table-tucked kitchen chairs. Every door
shut and wired. The cyclops eye of the alarm
staring out between the coats in the hall cupboard.
Time pulsing through the video clock.

Every window, save one in what had been
Richard's room at the back,
double-checked, closed and locked.

# Sunflower

Our sunflower has a sixty-degree slant,
and is falling into the grass.
September's rain and wind will bring it down,
tonight, later in the week.
It will happen, then
we shall see that it has happened.

The lower leaves, large brown hands,
hang limp and resigned. Its great
green gloved hands are sodden with rain.
They will weigh down the life of it, snap
the stem low where it has split.
It will fall to the slugs.

The child's painting
of a clown's funny, sad face
is blackened and turned down.
Ornamental, bird-feeder, oddball.
Sparrows and bees have worried it to death
and the head, heavy with seed, can barely pull
towards the last of the light.

Everything on this day, in this place,
hinges on our showy, singular, sad sun.
Now the sumac has flames of red and yellow,
birds have broken their August silence
and a squirrel interrupts the aspens,
working its way on airy tracks down the garden
to the apples of autumn.
Our sunflower is falling into the grass.

# The Spill

After days of rain on the course
each bunker has black and blue
shapes drawn in its sand.
Something has been washed and rises

to glint polished black in the sun.
This stuff dredged from the Channel,
brought for cheapness, carries grains
from a century of coal.

Mardy, Britannia, Ferndale,
Maritime, Parc and Dare,
Nantgawr, Bargoed Steam,
Senghennydd, Lady Windsor.

All that power firing the Empire,
two world wars, spilled from the ships
and their loading — ghosts under
the big rise and fall of the western sea.

As we line up our shots on the fifth hole
the distant, dazzling sea is a silver divide:
black coal built the Welsh side,
black chained muscle built the English.

I punch my ball out of the sand
and before putting the iron back in my bag
spit on the club face and wipe away
the grooves' black dust with my hand.

# Keeping Score

Two days ago at the 10th
both short of the pond with our drives,
we stopped to watch the four ducks
— three ducks and a drake, you said —
tail-tipping under the water,
and a solitary moor-hen
with its white breast stripe.

I played over with a careful 8;
you caught the fifth bunker of your round with a 7,
fluffed your first, then hacked out
in an angry sand storm.
You sank a monster down the steep green
while I pitched and ran mine on with a 9
and left it dead.

The hole was halved —
you with 5
and me with a 5:
your flukey 5
and my neat 5.
Still two up
with eight to play.

From the tee on the 11th
we watched three ducks splash
out of the water and into the air.
And a drake and the coot,
*fulica atra*, with the white breast stripe,
had the pond to themselves.

# Gorse at the Seventh

Tricked again by Christmas,
this mild mid-December spell,
above the green
the south-facing gorse puts out
its strings of yellow flowers.
Tight and sharp, they glint
like candles against the spiky bushes
under the grey end-of-day sky.

A Concorde sounds its booms overhead,
but I know that trick and must look further west
where the silver dart
is already miles along the line,
chasing the sun to New York.
Celebs and the rich popping over to shop
or do the last business of the year —
politics and Donna Karan.

The booms fade away and the traffic
noise is rubbed out by a lift of wind.
A chill end to things with the gorse
flowers cold and waxy
between their angled spikes.
Then a bank of flattened bracken moves
to become a cock pheasant, his eye
above the bright ruff catching mine.

This could be the end of it — a mile
from the clubhouse, the course empty
and the light draining away.
Already street lamps are glowing
into life, the headlights of distant cars,
the airport shaped only by its lit windows.
On the last two holes I'll have to be straight
or lost. No one would know. Not a soul.

# The Swing

I never understood
the relaxed, open secret of it —
how Arthur Booker, my schoolteacher,
could slowly wind up his swing and
stroke the ball down the fairways
between the treacherous dunes of sand,
those clinging, vicious, salty grasses.

You have to reach that time,
it might be fifteen or fifty,
when you know the game-playing to be
a circle of solipsism and dream,
a willing suspension of disbelief.
A brittle magic circle held in by the road,
the dunes, the railway, or trees, or the fence,
and the blue, blue, changing blues of the sea
                              and sky.
The place we go to figure ourselves differently,
play at time, using it against sense.
The place where, as Shankly said,
it's not a matter of Life and Death,
it's more important than that.

For a time.
And Arthur Booker's silky swing, that
thing of unforced strength, clearly
showed me that. It's taken forty years
to recognise it as metaphor and fact.

So, address the ball. Aim straight.
Follow through and don't look
for the result until the head is shouldered
up and your eyes know where to look
before they look. Wait.
Use what skill you have
and call it fate.

# Archaeology of the Fifth

Even a straight drive and second shot
leaves you on a down or up slope at the fifth.
There's no fair lie: are those
the workings of an old lead mine
by the tee at the end of the lane?

In 'forty-one a Heinkel swinging
from the ack-ack around the docks
had taken enough and banking to the west
dumped his load and cratered this patch.
The officers billeted in The Bothy heard
them go off — "Bloody close!"

A pilot leaned into the stick,
the bomb aimer's thumb one second
from obliterating two farms, and Wenvoe St. Mary's
where Normans prayed, Wesley preached.
Unburdened, faster, up to speed,
did that plane make it back to France?

Or did a boy that day in his Spitfire
over the South Coast spot a straggler,
and coming at him out of the blinding sun,
add them to his score? Gravity and chance.

When they re-built the bunkers in ninety-nine
they hit a trench of telephone cables.
Military police paid a visit. Something
from the air-base at St Athan to somewhere else.
Hush it. The Cold War. Bunkers.
Gravity and chance are all.

You play an eight iron at the pin
but that prevailing south-west wind
sweeps up the rise of the sixth and catches
the hang of your ball, which can't grip
the saucer's edge of the green, falling
away from the flag and down the slope.

# Eclipses

When I was nine, there was a partial eclipse.
We were marched into the yard of Pentreporth School
with our failed photo negatives to dim the glare.
That's clearer to me now than the hospital stare
I gave the full thing the other week.
Perhaps my memory's playing the fool
Or is it that we paste and edit,
working light from the black?

Where did I see the second full eclipse
of this spoiled and tired century?

Cardiff. The Heath Hospital. Fourth floor.
Meningitis. With safety glasses bought
for the French chateau we'd planned,
further along its arc over northern Europe.
A totally eclipsed sun — too obvious a metaphor
for what I was going through.

Further west, at the other end of Wales,
a pin-prick away, you and Mary
stood in your back gardens, Mum,
just looking up at your second eclipse.

You remember the first — June 1927,
when you were nine:
all the people from the back-to-backs
climbed up Bicester Hill, just after dawn.
Your father had taken a cracked pane,
held and turned it carefully over a candle
and smoked it evenly to a safe dark.

You won't remember the black sun that day
but can still recall the excited street
and your father's magic of the smoked glass
changing the world to grey.

# Leonids

Gone midnight, I rise
to view the promised Leonids.
Nothing.

Under a low cloud cover
that blankets the sky
at all points of the compass,
nothing.

Not a star, no moon,
just a dullness,
the street-lamps fuzzy in the thick dampness.

Once every thirty-three years
the meteor's myriad sparks
shower onto our atmosphere and dance
light down to us in ostentatious display.
It is calculable, predictable, but appears
as random as chance.

This year they strike and spark
out of sight.
I'll not see them now.
The coincidence of this planet's curve
and that shining debris.

With clocks and calendars we measure
all the living moves.
In Vermont and Pembrokeshire
years ago, I remember
seeing shooting stars —
surprising and random they seemed.
And cold.

Back under the duvet
you've warmed a cave,
my love,
where dreams of flight unfold.

# Eggs

How your childhood is pieced together.
This Christmas he tells you about
your grandfather
out at night with three caps —
one for his head against the weather,
and one slipped over each boot,
so that he left no print in the snow
across the farmyard to the chickens.
As quiet as snow itself,
under the cracked moon
his hands slipping softly
into the warm, drowsy nests.
And the polished ochre eggs bursting
their bright suns in the morning pan,
one secret and one secret and another.

# Glyn

When asked if he believed in God
"Often," he said.
But when I went to see him
the day before he died
there was no sign of light.
Sitting pillowed in bed
he was exhausted by the fight.

We talked of Wales, and friends
and literature,
what was left to write.
I held his left hand
worn as ninety-year-old leather
and tried not to look
at the stump of his other
phantomed in his folded pyjama sleeve.
His eyes were empty and wet.
His hand, light as a feather,
gripped mine like a child's
when I rose to leave.

We were in Boston when we heard he'd died,
but saw the interment of his ashes
two weeks later
in Llansteffan, that small village church
at the mouth of the Towy,
a stone's throw from Fern Hill.
Friends smiled, friends cried.
A Christian gentleman gone before.

Now with Jan cut down suddenly by that virus,
a sixth-former with cancer in his marrow,
our neighbour's mind gone senile,
we see the business of living in this world
goes on making little sense.
It's all we've got, still.
The hand that holds at the end,
the words we've written and read.
When asked if he believed in God,
"Often," he said.

# Three Dolmens

## I

## Maes-y-Felin

On Midsummer's Eve
The stones of this chamber
Rise, and move through the dark
To bathe in the river.
So death is washed
From their stone memory.
They spin three times
And settle again into their shelter-shape.
But each Hallowe'en
Those who dare come to this place
Are granted anything they wish.

When some hundreds of men
Gathered to raise this capstone
They could have known nothing of forty
Square yards, or forty tons,
Or any measurement,
But only that the hunters of three huts
Broke their backs, three women
And their children then starved.
Nine corpses laid in the crow-grave
Until the bones grew white,
When crushed, filled as many red clay pots
In the dark cave they'd made
In the middle of the thickest wood,
In the middle of the greenest meadow.

## II

### Gwal-y-Filiast

On May Day, St. John's Day
Or Midwinter Day,
He who would stay
Alone but one night
At this ancient site
Will surely suffer one fate of three —
To die, go stark mad, or a poet be.

This field was cursed for generations
— Some darkness, some unrecorded evil —
And nothing grew or prospered in that place,
Despite the good rain, the sea-air
Freshening from the distant Channel.
Fit only for a kennel of greyhounds
And their bitches, and farm-hands whispering
To other bitches there and groans
And licking of the face.

To the south a huddle of women
Turned to stone for dancing
On the holy day
Hold their places in the sun.

# III
## The King's Quoit

Proud now on the headland path
Overlooking the bright yellow wedge of sand,
This place would first have been earth-covered,
Chosen further inland, closed and dry
And thousands of memories before
Gerald of Wales and his castle across the bay.
What a fine place to rest your crushed bones —
The unmapped, endless Atlantic washing in,
Smoothing out footprints of the corpse-bearers
In the drying sand.

A handful of coves eastwards
Was where I threw my father's ashes
Towards the sea.
A fine August day of empty, blue heavens.
They fell on heather and gorse and lichen
Haphazard.

       Though now I see the sense
Of chambers, the thousands of muscle-labours,
The earth-works engineering, the twined ropes,
The log-rollers, the burned props,
The ice-cleaved slabs, the intuited point of balance —
The cap-stone, the pillars, the piled earth darkness,
The grave-cave, the death-womb.

## Acknowledgements

Acknowledgements are due to the editors of the following publications where some of these poems first appeared: *The Cimarron Review*, *The Interpreter's House*, *The David Jones Journal*, *Dal Confine: Scelte Poesie/Selected Poems* (Moby Dick, Italy), *The Literary Review*, *The New Orleans Review*, *Over Milk Wood*, *The Poetry Review*, *Poetry Ireland Review*, *Poetry Wales*, *Planet*, *Scintilla*, *Slope*, *Thumbscrew*, *Wading Through Deep Water* (Coychurch Press).

I am grateful to the University of Glamorgan for continued support. And, of course, my family: *Eggs* and *Leonids* are especially for Margaret, *Eclipses* for my mother. Gareth and Bronwen's energy drives the *Amherst Letters*.